QUADCOPTER AND DRONE PHOTOGRAPHY

How to Move Your Photography Business or Hobby to the Next Level

Contents

Introduction

"For all of human history our perspective has basically been stuck at eye-level and now for the first time in history, we can see the world the way the birds do."

—*Chris Anderson, 3D Robotics*

As a full-time mental health professional it is part of who I am to consistently explore new perspectives, and I expect that was my main motivation to venture into the world of aerial photography.

But I could not have imagined that what would start out as a simple curiosity would soon turn into a passion. As I learned more and more about this growing field of technology and art that allowed me to gain new ways of looking at things, I wanted to share it with others. And so this book was developed.

My approach is different from those who speak strictly from a technological point of view, although I do address those practicalities. But an underlying theme of this guide is the usefulness of being able to do creative work as an exciting new business opportunity or as an intriguing hobby.

With the investment of a few hundred dollars you can join the fascinating world of aerial radio-controlled drone and quadcopter photography. You can learn how to capture both stills and videos from unique perspectives and offer a wide range of new services to businesses.

In this guide you will learn the basics of what you need to set up your own aerial photography business as well as how to market yourself. We will talk about how this new way of doing things translates into new business opportunities.

We will also provide you with details about the rules and regulations that govern aerial photography and the changes that are expected in the near future. You will learn the ways you and others can stay safe when you launch your cameras into the air.

1

You will discover that you can spend as much or as little as you wish to establish yourself in this business. Generally speaking, spending about $1,000 will get you well on your way in this field. We will offer guidelines on equipment and accessories in different price ranges.

According to the Center for the Study of the Drone, the Federal Aviation Administration of the United States predicts that by 2018 there will be about 7,500 drones flying over the country.

One of the reasons drones have had a sudden spurt in popularity is that the technology now available is making it easier to present units to the public in an affordable price range. The processors, radios, GPS technology, gyros, accelerometers and magnetometers are for the most part no different than those used in our own smart phones.

They open up new horizons for photographers. Our line of sight is extended past where our feet will take us; our perspective is enlarged to include a clear view from above as we look down at our earth, and our safety is protected as we take pictures of marshlands and bogs without wading into them.

At the end of this guide, we have included a Bonus Section with details on some of the best websites to check out for more information and to see what other people are doing in this field.

Although aerial photography accomplished with drones is not new, it is becoming more accessible and that is making a world of difference. For the first time in our history, it is possible for the average small businessperson to venture into the field.

Paul Virilio, a cultural theorist, once described flying as more than a new way of looking at things. He suggested it was the "ultimate way" of seeing.

Now we all have a chance to view our world from that privileged viewpoint.

How to Select the Drone that is Best for You

The concept of attaching a camera to a drone and sending it into the sky so you can take some beautiful photographs can be a reality for a reasonable investment.

Drones got their name from the U.S. military who used the word to describe any machine that flew without a person at the controls.

Here is a quick guide for finding the drone that fits your creative needs and your budget.

Drones are unmanned aerial vehicles that you control from the ground. The average drone is composed of light composite materials. It is thus light enough to fly easily but strong enough to survive at high altitudes.

Drones come in versions from four prop to six prop to eight prop and can take cameras from the smallest compact to the top of the line DSLR. They get their power from rechargeable batteries and can usually stay up for between five to 15 minutes, depending on the model and size.

A few drones can stay up for 20 minutes, and just recently Ehang Guangshi Technology Company Ltd. (EHANG) came out with a Black Ghost model that runs for 30 minutes. In addition, their premium drone the Skyway, which retails for $5,000, can stay up for 50 minutes. EHANG is a technology enterprise founded by investors from China, the United States and Singapore.

When you go drone shopping, key considerations are motors and propellers. For aerial photography, you want something with the smallest possible vibration so you can shoot steady videos.

Most drones, especially those on the lower end of the price range, will be radio-controlled consoles with joysticks that are used for setting their speed, direction and height. At the high end of the unmanned aerial systems (UAS) option is the Parrot AR Drone 2.0 which can actually be controlled with an app on your iPad or iPhone.

Do your research before you go drone shopping and try to get feedback from fellow photographers who have the same requirements as you for their businesses. I will also be making some recommendations throughout the book, and I want to stress from the start that I receive no remuneration from any company to mention their products.

I suggest that you start off with an AR Parrot Drone 2.0 that costs about $300. What I really like about this type of drone is that as soon as you charge and install its battery, it is recognized by your iPad immediately.

It has three other characteristics that are appealing for any "first" drone:

1. It needs only a small area to fly so you can experiment with it right in your neighborhood. You don't have to go through the process of packing it up and heading out of town to a big park. The advantage of this is that you can fly at a moment's notice and heighten your skills.

2. It compensates for your learning curve. It will hover easily and you can create user-defined flight ceilings which makes it less likely to lose as you hone your skills.

3. Finally, its flight controls are easy to learn.

Those are all the important characteristics to consider in selecting your initial drone.

Or, if you have no experience in flying drones whatsoever and you think you are going to crash a lot getting started, you might want to pick up something even cheaper, like the Hubsan X4 or the Estes ProtoX. They only stay up for about four minutes but you get a lot of experience learning how to control them.

The Hubsan X4, for example, is so small you will feel comfortable flying it around your living room, although it can also be flown outside. What makes it particularly good is that it has a coreless motor, which means it is a brushed motor but wound a little differently than the traditional brushed motor. That allows you to alter its RPM quicker than if it had a normal brushed motor. It can record HD video and runs about seven minutes before you have to recharge it for 40 minutes.

If you want to go middle of the line, try a quadcopter like the popular DJI Phantom 2 for about $700. It has some nice options including GPS positioning and a nice compact camera mount. I personally found this quadcopter the easiest unit to learn to use. What is great about it is that it was specifically designed for photography and has a hookup for a GoPro camera. The Phantom 2 Vision + comes with its own camera and video transmission system. It will stay up for about 20 minutes.

If you really want to treat yourself, however, consider one of the high quality multi-rotors, such as the Infinit Jib model which can carry sufficient equipment to take the quality of film that could end up in a movie. These start around $9,000 and extend all the way up to the top of the line version of around $30,000.

Another fine option is the DJI Inspire, I which can fly up to 50 miles per hour and weighs just 6 ½ pounds. On one battery charge it can stay airborne for up to 20 minutes. You can add one of these to your collection for about $3,500. What I love about this model is that it is GPS enabled, meaning that when it is hit with a gust of wind it automatically corrects itself and stays still for photography. Even nicer is that when you are done, all you have to do is press a button and it returns to you.

In the range between $1,500 and $3,000, the DJI Flame Wheel F450 (quad) is a nice option. What I especially like about it is that the camera is mounted in the front so the propellers never end up in your photo or video. The 3D Robotics Y6 and X8 models are powerful drones as well.

Tips for Taking Amazing Aerial Photographs

A combination of research and practice builds a solid foundation for enhancing your skills in aerial photography.

Before I started to take my own aerial photographs, I poured over numerous websites that showed some amazing shots taken from drones. They gave me inspiration, ideas and perspective on what was possible.

If you are just starting, I encourage you to do the same thing. For example, take a minute and look at the winning entries from the aerial photography contest of *National Geographic:*

http://voices.nationalgeographic.com/2014/07/11/winners-of-first-drone-aerial-photo-contest-announced/

The next thing that I discovered was something I should have guessed, but I was completely surprised. The fact is, it isn't all that easy to fly a drone.

A quadcopter, for example, will go up and down but also backwards and forwards and all degrees in between. Think about it being more than 100 feet in the air and it's not hard to get disoriented. You think you are pushing the joystick forward, but it ends up veering sideways. You think you are going to go sideways and it starts to come down like a rock.

You have to get very accustomed to the controls and appreciate their sensitivities. Coupled with that, you have to factor in the force of gravity, and we haven't even mentioned the wind yet.

Personally, the first time I tried to fly it I did it in my basement. I figured that at least I wouldn't lose it, and if it crashed, it wouldn't be too badly damaged. It was a good idea because I quickly realized I had a lot to learn.

From there I graduated to a large field early in the morning when there were no people or animals around. All in all, I would have to say it was about a week and a half before I felt really comfortable and in control of my drone, and longer than that to say I felt really accomplished at flying it.

This is the time I also realized that it would be good to have some spare parts, like an extra battery, replacement propellers and replacement gears. For the small quad I was experimenting with they were cheap, and by having them on hand I could continue with my practice sessions uninterrupted. Most of the parts were really easy to replace.

I knew that if I wanted to take good pictures with my drone camera, I would have to be able to fly steadily and in the area and direction I wanted to go.

Here are eight other tips I have gathered from trial and error and from talking with fellow photographers.

1. Put your drone in GPS mode. A big problem with aerial photography is keeping pictures and videos from being shaky and blurred from motion. If your drone has a GPS mode, turn it on to take your photos. Once the drone is at the proper location, release the manual controls and turn on the GPS mode. It will help to stabilize the machine and let it hover as steadily as possibly. A clearer, more in-focus photo will be the result.

2. Go up a little higher. When you start to take aerial photos, your natural tendency is to want to get really close to what you are photographing. You want to look directly into the face of the mountain. It is only when you go higher and move a little further away that you realize how much grander your photo is, because what you are seeing is now in perspective to the world around it. Increase your altitude and you will often end up with a better photo.

3. Don't ignore the weather. If you are just starting out and you haven't purchased an expensive drone, pay particular attention to the wind. Make your photo excursions on calmer days, not days when the wind will rock you out of focus.

4. Align vertical and horizontal frames with your camera. Aerial photography gives you a unique opportunity to capture the patterns of our planet, from cornfields to gardens to islands dotting an ocean. Your shot will be more effective if you align your camera vertically when you see a vertical pattern and horizontally when you see a horizontal pattern. What is going to be most striking in the end is the angles in any pattern and this little trick will make the most of them.

5. Time your photo taking with the sun. If you take aerial shots with the sun directly behind you, they will appear flat. You will find your best shots are taken either early in the morning or later in the afternoon when the sun's angles are most effective at enhancing what is on the ground.

6. When shooting videos, make sure you use a gimbal. This is the pivoted support that allows your camera to rotate fully around a single axis. When you are shooting video, it will help to stabilize your image.

7. You can capture the wind. The age-old question of how you can photograph something as fleeting and invisible as the wind can be answered in aerial photography. You can illustrate the wind in your scene by showing the movement in trees and objects in the foreground of your photo or video. But remember, don't fly when the wind is really high. Anything stronger than 20 miles per hour is trouble.

8. Watch the altitude – Many of us have found out the hard way that extremely high altitudes can seriously impact our drones. Many of the lower end models have a tendency to endure frozen motors when they are flying at particularly high altitudes where the air is really thin and cold. It's another reminder to really keep an eye on your environment when you go out flying your drone.

Making Sure you Comply with FAA Regulations

As you embrace your new hobby or business in aerial photography, it is important to get started on the right foot by ensuring you comply with regulations established by the United States Federal Aviation Administration (FAA).

If you are not operating in the United States, check with the government body that regulates air traffic in your country. Most countries have special regulations that apply to drones.

In the U.S., it is permissible to mount a camera on a radio-controlled aircraft and take pictures or videos for your personal use. At this time, however, you are not allowed to charge a fee for taking those photos or to sell them to someone else, or promote your aerial photography as a business. That is considered commercial use and it is currently prohibited.

If you are caught doing that, you will likely get a cease-and-desist letter from FAA. There is potential for legal action in certain cases.

For hobbyists, there are also rules to follow. You must fly below 400 feet and notify your nearest airport operator if you are flying within three miles of an airport.

All of that is about to change.

The FAA, acknowledging that it does not wish to smother the emerging industry of aerial photography, has just announced a new set of proposals that will regulate the industry, but still allow it to move forward.

According to a news release issued by the FAA, the new proposed rules contain these key elements:

1. All unmanned aerial systems (UASs) including drones and quadcopters weighing less than 55 pounds and travelling less

than 100 miles per hour (87 knots) maximum speed are covered under the proposed regulations.

2. Operators of these UASs will not need to have a traditional FAA airman certificate, but they will need to pass an initial aeronautical knowledge test at an FAA-approved knowledge-testing center. This process is estimated to cost about $300. As part of this process, you will also be subject to a security check, but there is no fee attached to that.

3. Operators cannot fly if they knowingly have any physical or mental condition that would interfere with the safe operation of their UAS.

4. You can only fly your UAS in daylight hours where there is at least three miles of visibility and with clouds at or above 500 feet above ground level.

5. Operators will be allowed to fly in certain contained airspaces (Classes B, C, D and E) with prior air traffic control clearance.

6. A small UAS does not require an FAA airworthiness certificate but must be registered.

7. Most importantly, specific commercial operations will be permitted, including crop monitoring, research and development, educational uses, power-line/pipeline inspection in hilly or mountainous terrains, antenna inspections, aiding certain rescue operations, bridge inspections, aerial photography and wildlife nesting area evaluations.

Further information provided by the FAA makes it clear that the knowledge test will have to be done every two years and you will need to have an "operator's certificate" for the drone you are flying. They also clarify that an operator has to least 17 years of age.

These rules pertain to businesses only, not to hobbyists who come under another set of regulations.

While these proposed new regulations are a great first step in recognizing the legitimacy of the aerial photography business, among others, there are some disappointing aspects to them as well.

For example, they disallow autonomous flights, which means that you cannot just program your UAS and let it fly itself on a predetermined route or mission. You have to keep it in your visual line of sight at all times. You also cannot fly at night, which is when rock concerts and even some weddings take place.

Nonetheless, the economic potential is huge. The Association of Unmanned Vehicle Systems International, an industry trade association, suggests the annual economic benefit could surpass $100 million a year and create 70,000 jobs.

For instance, it is estimated that about 45,000 annual bridge inspections could be done by drones.

Just because these regulations are proposed, remember that they are not yet in place. It can take up to two years for proposed regulations to become actual laws. Supposing that the White House quickly approves the regulations, they will still have to be offered up for public comment, and the controversial nature of UASs means that could take quite a long time.

Currently the FAA bans all commercial drone flights with the exception of a few firms who have received waivers.

For hobbyists, some current rules involve flying no higher than 400 feet above ground level and never flying directly over people or vehicles. Steer away from all federal and state property like national parks, post offices, city halls and courthouses.

Stay five miles away from all airports. If someone expresses annoyance about your drone flying, land it and leave the area. Stay away from radio towers and power lines. Be aware that you are responsible for any damage caused by your drone. I recommend that you consider membership in The Academy of Model Aeronautics (http://www.modelaircraft.org/membership/membershipoptions.aspx) if you are just getting started. It offers a $58 a year membership that includes $2.5 million liability insurance coverage, certainly one of the best deals currently available.

Staying Safe in the Field with Aerial Photography

It is a happy coincidence that the best time for aerial photography is early in the morning and just as the day is wrapping up, since those are also the times of the day when there are fewer people around and small children and dogs are usually safe at home.

The important thing when you are flying drones is to ensure that you do not hurt anyone or yourself in the process. That is why you should never cavalierly fly your drone over the heads of people watching an event or just going about their business.

Watch out for dogs and cats and other small animals as well who will be upset with your drone or may try to race after it or capture it. During landing and takeoff be especially careful of dogs.

Never get so wrapped up in your art that you forget your equipment. Be mindful of the time remaining in your battery and set a personal timer if necessary. Set it at least five minutes before you think you need it to give yourself time to finish a shot you are setting up and still get your drone back on time.

Practice and become competent with your drone before you take it outside and fly it.

In response to requests from the public concerned about drones flying overhead the U.S. Civil Aviation Authority came up with its own list of safety guidelines. They suggest that a drone fitted with a camera should not be flown over or within 150 meters of any congested area or over or within 150 meters of any organized outdoor event like a concert or sporting event.

It should also not be flown within 50 meters of any vessel, vehicle or building that is not under the control of the person flying the drone, and within 50 meters of any person except during take-off or landing.

It must also not be flown within 30 meters of any person except for the person in charge of it.

The FAA also advises that drones should not be flown through fireworks. It is dangerous for two reasons: it can damage the drone in such a way that it cannot be landed safely and it could divert a pyrotechnic downward to the crowd viewing the display.

Beware of flying near high voltage lines, trees or buildings and stay away from magnetic fields which can impact the drone's operation. Don't allow sand and dust to penetrate it.

Do not land your drone on water or a wet surface.

The remote pilot ultimately has the responsibility for ensuring that the flight can be conducted safely.

How to Tap the Potential of your Aerial Photography or Video Business

One of the first entrepreneurs to fully appreciate the value of an aerial photography business was George R. Lawrence who operated at the turn of the last century.

His motto was inspiring. He promised his clients he could deliver "the hitherto impossible" in his photography business.

He did this by building one of the first drones used for aerial photography. He built a train of 17 kites attached to a piano wire cable from which a camera was suspended. It was mounted on a stabilizing mechanism he had constructed.

He was also one of the first photographers to made real money from this kind of work. His famous aerial photography of San Francisco after the 1906 earthquake yielded him about $15,000 in sales, which would be the equivalent of around $370,000 today.

Yet his determination and innovation continue to inspire a new generation of aerial photographers determined to make a living from taking pictures from flying drones.

Industry experts are currently predicting that the use of drone photography will amount to billions of dollars in business over the next few years. In a report released in October, 2014, Lux Research of Boston suggested the business of unmanned aerial vehicles will climb to about $1.7 billion by the year 2025.

Drones are also being used by the pipelines and power industry to inspect their communication towers and wind turbines.

In this chapter we will look at potential customers for your new business. Some of them, like real estate agents and wedding planners, may be obvious, but have you considered farmers and mountain climbers in your list of possible clients?

People in the agricultural industry are turning to drones as a way to photograph crops. This is an affordable means for the farmer to secure information that was previously just not available or was too expensive to secure. By having crop photos taken they can conduct more detailed analyses, determine different growing patterns, see areas impacted with pests, and other valuable information.

Drone photography is also becoming in demand as a means of capturing images of adventure sports such as mountain climbing. In 2012, for example, a group of Swiss climbers used it to get photos of climbers scaling the Karakoram, a challenging mountain range. Surfers and skiers in remote locations will now also be able to obtain photographs of themselves in action at some of their most demanding moments. Even mountain bikers have hired drone photographers recently to get footage of them working their way down mountain trails at high speeds.

Other sports that can be captured by drones include kayaking, track and field and even hiking. At the 2014 Winter Olympics in Sochi, drone photography was used to record snowboarding and skiing competitions.

Just recently, the $1,149 Hexo +, a self-flying drone, was profiled in *Men's Journal*. It will allow athletes like joggers or hikers to map out their flight plan on their smart phone, then set up the drone in "follow me" mode and attach a GoPro and you can obtain footage of yourself running or walking along.

Meanwhile, real estate aerial photography has already started to be a mainstream component of any photography business, and that will just continue to grow in the months to come. For high-end properties set amid expertly landscaped settings or in wilderness locations, aerial photography will be a must to sell the property.

In one shot, the potential seller can immediately see that the house has a pool, the number of outbuildings, and gardens without having to click through a couple of dozen photos. Realtors have long wanted that one special shot that will stop potential buyers in their tracks with its magnificence, but it was too costly in the past to hire helicopters and planes. Now that the process has become more affordable, they are beating down the doors to hire aerial photographers.

Filmmakers are also potential clients as are operators of wilderness patrols like forest rangers and search and rescue organizations. Drone photography has already been proven useful in the search for missing people.

Weddings held in natural settings like beaches, cliff-tops and gardens can be beautifully captured with aerial photography, and this is one area that will continue to increase as more and more examples become available. In the same way that videos became an option that couples added on to their still photos and albums without even blinking, so will aerial photography in the future.

Rock concerts, dog and horse shows, county fairs and parades also have potential for aerial photography. As soon as the new regulations are in place, enterprising photographers should seek contracts with municipalities for aerial footage that can be streamed onto their websites for big events. They are already streaming webcams in many cases; this is just one more dimension to add.

Because drones can be outfitted with surveillance equipment, they will be an obvious asset for law enforcement agencies. Photographers knowledgeable about aerial photography may find these agencies to be excellent clients for new work in everything from photographing grow operations to crime scenes.

While the new regulations coming this year (2015) are expected to make running a business easier, it is still a complicated area. At this point, most commercial photographers tell their clients that they are not being charged for the actual taking of the aerial photographs but they will be charged for photo editing. It is a subtle difference that keeps most of them from receiving cease-and-desist orders from the FAA.

How to Market Yourself to Gain New Aerial Photography Clients

You may see a need for aerial photography in the business world, you may have identified potential customers, and you may have honed your skills in this field, but to succeed you will need to make that link between yourself and the customer. That involves marketing.

In the same way that you will take your time to determine the equipment you will use and become skillful using it, you must also take the time to determine how you want to market your business when the new regulations are passed.

It is easy to advise new entrepreneurs to just run out and set up a website, post their profiles on social media sites and get going, and there's certainly a component of all of that which needs to be done. But you will be ill-served and setting yourself up for failure if you do not spend as much time on your business plan as on your equipment plan.

Before you can start to market you must decide what kind of client you want to focus on, where they will likely see your message, and what kind of message will appeal to them. Then you are ready to build your marketing strategy.

As an entrepreneur myself, I know it is important in every business to determine from the start what makes you unique from all the others in your field. Do you bring added value to the table? Do you have a specialty that others don't have? Do you keep your investments so reasonable that you are able to keep your prices reasonable and target a larger group of potential clients? In other words, what kind of a business do you really want to operate?

One piece of literature that I found to be particularly helpful in these early stages of consideration was Guy Kawasaki's video on "Writing an Effective Mission Statement." You can access it at http://www.entrepreneur.com/video/219952.

If you need to set up a new website, you can create that for free on sites like www.WordPress.com or http://www.weebly.com/. Take the time to create good content that lets readers know what makes you unique in your field, what services you can offer them, and examples of your work. Writing regular blogs or even occasional longer articles on your site is another useful tool to establish your expertise on the subject and build your clientele.

Next, make sure you create a Facebook page for your business, a LinkedIn profile for yourself and your business, and join any other social media sites that might specifically be seen by your potential clients.

When you are a small entrepreneur it is important to not spread yourself too thin. Set up a strategy that you can reasonably handle and maintain, and do not try to tap into every single option that is available.

Set aside specific times during your week to maintain your marketing efforts. There is nothing more detrimental than to have a website that shows a portfolio with the last offering about five years ago. Your clients want to see what you are doing now, and the only way you can do that is to conduct regular updates.

If you need help with your blog or White Papers, you can usually obtain reasonably priced assistance from sites like www.elance.com.

Treat Yourself to Some Accessories for Your Drone

Chances are that you purchased a drone with a camera included in the package to get started, but if you didn't, look especially at the GoPro Inc. line of cameras that are eminently suited to be mounted on drones. These cameras are widely used for extreme action videos and will take both stills and videos in high definition.

The GoPro Hero 3 Black Edition, weighing in at 73 grams, is an excellent choice because it records video at 45 Mbps and has built-in WiFi for downloading the footage.

As you grow your expertise, however, you will find that there is an endless array of other cameras and accessories available to help you move to the next level of professionalism.

For example, I recommend the purchase of first-person view (FPV), sometimes sold as remote-person view. It gives me extra control over my drone. I can pilot it remotely from my own perspective using the mounted camera which is fed wirelessly back to my video goggles. It can also be fed to your video monitor.

What I would like to get in the near future is the pan-and-tilt gimbaled camera which has a senor in the goggles allowing me to use two on-board cameras so I can enjoy a totally stereoscopic view.

A vibration isolator is another key accessory for taking professional photographs from your drone. It works by isolating the vibration between the drone and the mount. When you are shooting videos in particular, vibration is your enemy. There are many vibration isolators on the market. AAC, for example, offers silicone gel bolt mounts specifically designed for UAVs and quadcopters.

You will also need a gimbal if one does not come with your package. Gimbals are gadgets that will allow you to mount things to your drone, from compact cameras to large telescopes. A single-axis gimbal head is used to permit the balanced movement of camera and lenses. Large gimbal mounts like two or three axis altitude mounts are most useful in satellite photography. A gimbal can be bolted to the bottom of your drone and can hold your GoPro camera.

A number of companies sell video transmitters to increase your range, but be careful that you do not violate regulations by allowing your drone to get too far away from you. If you want to risk it, you can look at an analogue video transmitter that will broadcast video from your camera to you. A popular model is the Immersion RC 5.8 GHz (600 mw).

If you have the budget, another good purchase is an anti-gravity motor which will perform better than the stock motors that come with most drones. The anti-gravity motor will give you greater speed and longer flying times because it turns at a higher revolution. I love it because it is maintenance free, not like a stock motor that needs to be disassembled and regularly maintained. Another plus is that its bearings stay lubricated for the life of the motor.

Still another valuable upgrade is to invest in carbon fiber propellers as opposed to the regular plastic ones that usually come on your drone. What makes the carbon ones so much better is that they are more efficient, they vibrate less, and their extra rigidity keeps them from warping and bending. With carbon fiber propellers, your drone will be able to go faster and negotiate harder maneuvers.

Looking for Innovative Lenses and Filters to Enhance your Work

As aerial photography through drones grows in popularity, the camera industry is moving forward to offer intriguing new lens options to help photographers capture unique pictures of our world.

For example, a system established by Panasonic and Olympus in 2008 is about to be fitted in 2015 onto drones made by DJI. Called the Micro Four Thirds System, it is an interchangeable lens standard that will allow aerial photographers to make use of a variety of lenses ranging from telephoto, to wide angle and to single focal length.

Just recently a team of U.S. researchers constructed a unique camera that will allow for an almost 180-degree field of view through the use of hundreds of minute lenses.

The lens is a duplicate of the natural lens found in the eyes of bark beetles and fire ants. It is anticipated that it will be developed for use with drone photography as well as with medical technology.

When shopping for lenses to be used in aerial photography, remember that a shorter lens works better, especially on windy days when the wind will catch a longer lens and move it about. Fixed focal length lenses are effective.

Cameras on drones will provide better pictures with faster lenses like an f2.9 lens. You need fast shutter speeds of around 1/1000 of a second at 200 mm.

Keep in mind as well that the drone's landing gear could be impacted if the lens is shorter than a 35 mm lens on a 35 mm camera. A DSLR needs at least a 25 mm lens.

Meanwhile, you can also take your landscape aerial photography to the next level with any of the vast array of lens filters currently on the market. With the skillful use of different filters you can take an ordinary photo and make it extraordinary. You can focus on unique colors and textures and add dimension and atmosphere.

Some photographers find the number of available lenses so overwhelming that they decide to keep it simple and natural and not use them at all. In the case of aerial photography that is a mistake, since certain lenses are essential in clearing up problems that are unique to this kind of work.

For example, you can reduce glare with polarizing filters, you can lengthen your exposure time with neutral density filters and you can make different color corrections with a range of different colored filters.

The filters can be purchased as either screw-on or front filters, and both have specific advantages. The front filters are more flexible while screw-on lenses stay in place as long as they match the size of your lens.

Whenever you use filters in aerial photography or any other kind, you need to be aware that they will impact your image and they could produce a negative result in the quality of the image since they put another layer of glass between the landscape and your camera's sensor.

Here is a list of some common filters and the ways they can best be used:

Magenta Drive Filter – When you are taking pictures of water reservoirs and fresh water lakes as well as salt water pools that appear green because of their algae content, a magenta drive filter can correct the color.

Polarizing Filter – Designed to reduce glare, the polarizing filter should be used with caution in aerial photography because it reduces how much light reaches the camera's sensor. If you pair it with your wide-angled lens, it can cause a distortion especially with sunsets, making them look very uneven and unrealistic. However, both circular and linear polarizers can be useful in taking pictures of the sky, water and woodlands because they improve color saturation.

Natural Density Filters – These are useful under circumstances where you need an extended time for exposure.

Gradual Neutral Density – These lenses assist photographers in controlling strong light. You will really have to experiment with this to make the most of it. The first time I used it I was shocked at how fast it blended from light to dark.

UV and Haze Filters – I am not a big fan of either one of these in aerial photography. I don't find they work the same as in regular photography. When you are shooting from your drone and there is a haze problem, you would be better off just using a red filter. However, their advantage is that they do protect the front of your camera lens.

Cool and Warm Filters – These two filter variations work to change the white balance of light that will be picked up by the sensor in the camera. You would use them on a day when you want to correct an unrealistic color cast or to add an element of warmth on a day that is totally cloudy. Once very popular and a mainstay in the standard photography bag, these two filters have been neglected of late since the advent of the digital camera. That is because the majority of those camera automatically make adjustments for white balance. However, they are often still used today for underwater photography.

How to Inject Creativity into your Aerial Photography

Physician and inventor Edward de Bono, who also wrote the book *Six Thinking Hats,* suggested that creativity is about breaking out of our established patterns of living and looking at the world in an entirely different way. He could have been predicting the rise of aerial photography with drones.

All of a sudden the world that the photographer's eye knew intimately has grown a new dimension. Instead of standing still and contemplating our shot, we must adjust to a device that twists and turns its way across our planet, leaving us with a myriad of impressions and confusion about just what to shoot.

We have to change the way that we think about planning all the elements of our shots.

The world of drone photography is new enough that there are not huge libraries full of advice and stories of the tried and true. Instead we are drawn together as a learning community in going out and seeing for ourselves just what we can create and interpret by looking top down at our world.

We see abstract patterns depicted in both brilliant and muted colors, nature's sculptures of sand and rock, and a horizon that taunts us to take a few more steps.

There is a tremendous joy in watching as we take an intimate journey across our land, experiencing its colors, textures, and spirits.

I encourage you to allow yourself the experience of stepping into this world without pre-conceived ideas. Instead, allow yourself to go through this sometimes smooth and sometimes bumpy ride with open curiosity.

Shoot wide, shoot often. Edit if you must, but allow yourself the experience of discovery and the education of making mistakes.

As with all new things, keep notes and journals recording the equipment used, lenses attached and the approaches to your work, so that both you and others can learn from this in the future.

Conclusion

The surge of photographers into aerial work is just beginning. As regulations change and the equipment becomes more and more affordable, you will be able to tap into this exciting new business and develop new perspectives on your business.

For our art and for our business, the results will be intriguing and may surpass a mere intellectual or economic exercise. We may actually be on the edge of yet another cultural revolution.

Throughout mankind's history there has always been a tremendous controversy between information and privacy. When Guttenberg invented the printing press around 1439, there were those in power who questioned what would happen to the order of society when ordinary people learned to read and have access to the literature of the world. The spread of knowledge always changes people as it did then.

The democratization of knowledge was brought full circle when the World Wide Web and home computers brought the wisdom of the ages and the answers for almost everything right into the homes of the ordinary person. A tap on our keyboard can make us knowledgeable about any subject.

Opponents to the spread of this information argued about the privacy implications, but their discontent was drowned out by the changing perspectives of people everywhere who saw their community expand from a few streets to an entire global village.

It is entirely possible that just as the computer democratized knowledge, the drone will democratize another dimension of our world: the sky. Throughout history we have looked up far more frequently than we have looked down.

Perhaps it is time to change our perspective and see how the world looks from this higher perspective. It is true that there will always be legitimate controversy about the possible intrusion of drones on privacy. These arguments will always be with us.

But there will be those artists who soar above them and capture images that are so spectacular that the rest of us all stop in our tracks and acknowledge that it was worth stretching our limits.

Enjoy exploring this new world!

Bonus Section

Want more information? Here are some great websites and links to more material on aerial photography and a chance to view what many creative people are doing in this field:

DIY Drones - http://diydrones.com/

This is a fun website of 30,000 members who gather online to share their mainly open-source designs.

Drone Flyers - http://www.droneflyers.com/

This is a website with comments and videos from drone flyers who share their discoveries and experiences.

Multi-Rotary Forums - http://multirotorforums.com/

This is a great online community where people share their work.

Center for the Study of the Drone at Bard College - http://dronecenter.bard.edu/about/

This site features the education and art community working together to furnish information about understanding drones. A key feature of this site is a regular blog that explores many aspects of drones.

Also featured on this site under "Publications" is a wonderful guide called "The Drone Primer: A Compendium of the Key Issues," a free download and a great read. To go directly to it, click:

http://dronecenter.bard.edu/publication/the-drone-primer/

Travel by Drone - http://travelbydrone.com/

Take a dronecation by watching wonderful video footage taken from drones from people all over the world who share them for everyone's enjoyment.

Drone Flying Demo - https://www.youtube.com/watch?v=0B-ZUu51xgM

GoPro Youtube – new videos each week - https://www.youtube.com/user/GoProCamera

DJI Phantom Users Group on Facebook - https://www.facebook.com/pages/DJI-Phantom-Users-Group/490340781006993

Dronestagram - http://www.dronestagr.am/

This is a community of drone photography enthusiasts who provide a platform for shared images and regularly sponsor contests

Aerial Horizon Photography - http://aerialhorizon.photography/

If you want to be inspired at what you are capable of doing with your drone and your camera, fill up your senses and spark your imagination with this site.

Got a second?

Thank you for purchasing and reading my book! I hope you enjoyed it and were able to gather some valuable information.

Can I ask a quick favor?

If you liked this book, I would really appreciate if you could take a minute or two to leave a review on Amazon. I love getting feedback from my readers and personally read all of my reviews.

This link will bring you right to the review page for this book: http:// amzn.to/1aYdAOi

Thanks!

Eric Hall